ESL/EFL Instruction for Intermediate Learners: Themed Vocabulary, Speaking, and Writing

Joseph Jensen is an experienced ESL/EFL language instructor with a Master's degree in education concentrating in ESL/EFL instruction from the University of Nebraska at Kearney.

With over 15 years of teaching experience in Japan, Joseph has taught English as a second language to students of all ages, ranging from young children to adults. In addition to teaching, Joseph has also developed curriculum for numerous schools and educational institutions, with a focus on creating engaging and effective lesson plans that cater to the needs of students from diverse backgrounds.

Be on the lookout for these books in this series.

- ESL/EFL Instruction for Beginner Learners: Themed Vocabulary, Speaking, and Writing
- ESL/EFL Instruction for Advanced Learners: Themed Vocabulary, Speaking, and Writing

Please consider subscribing to our Youtube channel to stay updated on new content.
https://www.youtube.com/@Globalearning_Academy

ESL/EFL Instruction for Intermediate Learners: Themed Vocabulary, Speaking, and Writing

Joseph Jensen

Globalearning

Brief Contents

Detail Contents

Detail Contents

Detail Contents

Detail Contents

About this Book

Teaching English as a second language (ESL) or foreign language (EFL) to any level of learners can be a complex and challenging experience. Unlike teaching in a native language, language teachers must deal with language barriers and constantly adapt their instruction to meet the needs of students from diverse backgrounds. As an ESL/EFL teacher, you must have a solid understanding of the English language and be able to communicate effectively in the language. However, your role as a language teacher goes beyond just language knowledge. You must also be well-versed in effective teaching strategies, curriculum design, and cultural sensitivity. You must have the ability to design lessons that cater to the individual needs and abilities of each student.

One of the biggest challenges of teaching ESL/EFL students is the need to help students understand all content areas, as opposed to traditional teachers who typically teach one subject. As an ESL/EFL teacher, you must help your students comprehend and communicate about a wide variety of subjects, such as science, history, and literature, in addition to teaching them the language itself. This can be a daunting task, as it requires not only language proficiency, but also an understanding of the content being taught. In addition, you must help students develop the language skills needed to navigate everyday situations, such as grocery shopping, going to the doctor, or conducting a job interview. This requires a deep understanding of the cultural context in which the language is used, as well as the ability to adapt your teaching style to meet the needs of students of all ages and backgrounds.

Another challenge of teaching ESL/EFL students is the need to be culturally sensitive and aware. Language is deeply intertwined with culture, and language teachers must be sensitive to the cultural backgrounds and experiences of their students. This includes understanding their values, beliefs, and customs, as well as their individual learning styles and preferences. Teachers must be able to address cultural differences in the classroom and create an inclusive and supportive learning environment for all students.

In addition to these challenges, ESL/EFL teachers must also stay current on the latest research and best practices in second language acquisition. They must be able to identify the learning style and language proficiency level of each student and design lessons that address their unique needs and learning goals. Unlike traditional subjects such as math or science, language learning is a dynamic and ongoing process that requires constant adaptation and adjustment. Teachers must be able to identify when students are struggling and provide additional support and guidance as needed.

In order to provide effective language input and promote language growth, teachers must be able to identify when students are struggling and provide additional support and guidance as needed. This is where having knowledge and understanding of the principles of second language acquisition becomes essential for ESL/EFL teachers. There are several hypotheses and methods related to second language acquisition, especially within the communicative approach to language instruction, including Dr. Stephen Krashen's Input Hypothesis, Dr. Merrill Swain's Output Hypothesis, and Dr. Rod Ellis and Dr. Susan Gass's Interactive methods.

Dr. Stephen Krashen's Input Hypothesis posits that language acquisition occurs when learners are exposed to language input that is comprehensible and just beyond their current level of understanding. This means that the language teacher must select materials and activities that are at an appropriate level for their students, but also provide some challenge to promote language growth. One way to achieve this is through the use of the "i+1" concept, where "i" represents the learner's current level of understanding and "+1" refers to the level of input that is slightly above their current level. For example, if a learner is at a beginner level, the teacher may provide input that is slightly more advanced than what the learner currently understands, but still comprehensible. This encourages the learner to stretch their language skills and acquire new vocabulary and grammar structures.

To implement the Input Hypothesis in the classroom, the teacher can use a variety of activities that provide comprehensible input and promote language acquisition. Some examples of such activities include:

- **Storytelling**: The teacher can tell stories using simple language and visuals to make the input comprehensible, and gradually introduce new vocabulary and grammar structures. This allows learners to acquire language in a natural and engaging way.
- **Reading**: The teacher can select reading materials

that are at the appropriate level for the learners, and provide support such as visual aids and context clues to make the input comprehensible. This helps learners to develop their reading skills and acquire new vocabulary and grammar structures.

- **Listening and speaking**: The teacher can use listening and speaking activities that are at an appropriate level for the learners, and provide opportunities for them to practice using new vocabulary and grammar structures. This allows learners to develop their oral communication skills and acquire language in a meaningful context.

Dr. Merrill Swain's Output Hypothesis complements Krashen's Input Hypothesis by emphasizing the importance of language production and output. According to this theory, learners need to use language in meaningful and communicative ways to develop their language skills. When learners produce language, they notice gaps in their knowledge and attempt to fill them through interaction and feedback from others. Therefore, language teachers must design activities that provide learners with opportunities to use the language actively and purposefully.

To implement this theory in the classroom, teachers can

incorporate various communicative tasks and interactive activities that encourage students to produce language in context. For example, teachers can organize group discussions on a topic, where students have to express their opinions, listen to others, and negotiate meaning. Another example could be role-playing, where students act out scenarios that involve using language in realistic situations, such as ordering food in a restaurant or negotiating a business deal. These types of activities provide learners with authentic and meaningful opportunities to use the language and receive feedback from their peers or teacher.

Feedback is a crucial element of the Output Hypothesis, as it enables learners to monitor and improve their language use. Teachers can provide feedback through error correction, clarifying misunderstandings, or encouraging students to use specific language structures or vocabulary. However, feedback should always be provided in a supportive and non-threatening way that helps students feel confident in their ability to use the language.

Rod Ellis and Susan Gass's Interactive methods are built around the concept of creating a rich and interactive language environment that allows for active participation and engagement from learners. This approach recognizes the importance of social interaction in language learning and emphasizes that learners acquire language through meaningful communication and collaboration with others.

One of the key elements of interactive methods is the use of group work and pair work activities. These activities provide learners with opportunities to practice their language skills in a supportive and interactive environment. For example, a language teacher might organize a group discussion on a topic relevant to the learners' interests or experiences, and then facilitate the discussion by asking open-ended questions and encouraging participation from all members of the group.

Another important aspect of interactive methods is the use of role-plays and simulations. Role-plays allow learners to take on different roles and engage in authentic communication in simulated real-world situations. This can be particularly effective for developing language skills related to specific contexts or situations, such as ordering food in a restaurant or negotiating a business deal.

Feedback is also a crucial element of interactive

methods. Learners need feedback to monitor their language use, identify areas where they need improvement, and make necessary adjustments to their language production. Feedback can come from the teacher, peers, or through self-reflection.

Paul Nation's Four Strands of Language Learning is a framework for designing language lessons that incorporate multiple aspects of language learning. These four strands are meaning-focused input, meaning-focused output, language-focused learning, and fluency development. By incorporating the principles of Krashen's Input Hypothesis, Swain's Output Hypothesis, and Ellis & Gass's Interactive Methods, language teachers can create lessons that incorporate all four strands of language learning.

The meaning-focused input strand involves providing learners with comprehensible input that is just beyond their current level of understanding. This can be achieved by selecting materials and activities that are appropriate for the learners' level, but also provide some challenge to promote language growth. Teachers can use Krashen's i+1 input principle to select materials and activities that are just beyond the learners' current level of proficiency. For example, a teacher might use authentic materials such as news articles, songs, or movies to expose learners to new vocabulary and grammatical structures.

The meaning-focused output strand involves giving learners the opportunity to use the language in meaningful and authentic ways. This can be achieved by creating opportunities for learners to engage with the language through communicative tasks and interactive activities, as emphasized by Swain's Output Hypothesis and Ellis and Gass's Interactive Methods. For example, a teacher might create a role-play activity in which learners have to use the language to negotiate and solve a problem together.

The language-focused learning strand involves explicitly teaching learners about the language, such as its grammar rules and vocabulary. This can be achieved through various techniques such as explicit instruction, error correction, and metalinguistic awareness activities. This strand is particularly important for learners who need more structured support in their language learning process.

The fluency development strand involves giving learners the opportunity to develop their fluency through activities that focus on developing automaticity and fluency in the language. This can be achieved through various techniques such as repetition, timed activities, and fluency-building exercises.

By incorporating all four strands of language learning into their lessons, language teachers can create a comprehensive and balanced approach to language learning that caters to the individual needs and abilities of their students.

This book, ESL/EFL Instruction for Intermediate Learners: Themed Vocabulary, Speaking, and Writing, provides a comprehensive resource for ESL/EFL teachers to incorporate all the principles we discussed earlier. The book is organized into 10 themes, with each theme including 50 targeted vocabulary words, 20 speaking prompts, useful phrases and idioms, 3 writing prompts, and an example classroom activity.

By providing targeted vocabulary words, the book aligns with Krashen's Input Hypothesis, as it ensures that the language input is comprehensible and just beyond the current level of understanding of the learners. The speaking prompts and writing prompts align with Swain's Output Hypothesis, as they allow learners to actively use language in a meaningful context and seek out ways to fill gaps in their knowledge. Additionally, the useful phrases and idioms provide learners with opportunities to use the language in authentic ways, consistent with Ellis & Gass's interactive methods. Finally, the example classroom activity for each theme provides a concrete example of how to combine all these principles into a single lesson, in accordance with Paul Nation's Four Strands of Language Learning. Teachers can use the book to plan and deliver effective lessons that cater to the individual needs and abilities of their students.

Here are some more detailed steps on how to use this book:

- Start by selecting a theme from the book, such as "health" or "entertainment."
- Review the 50 targeted vocabulary words provided for that theme and select the ones most appropriate for your students' level and needs.
- Use Krashen's Input Hypothesis to design activities and materials that provide comprehensible input just beyond your students' current level of understanding. For example, you might create a reading activity that includes some of the new vocabulary words, but also some familiar words to provide context.
- Use Swain's Output Hypothesis to design activities that encourage language production in a meaningful context. For example, you might design a speaking activity where students discuss their favorite foods or travel destinations using the new vocabulary words.
- Use Ellis and Gass's Interactive methods to create opportunities for student engagement and interaction. For example, you might design a group role-play activity where students plan a trip and use

the new vocabulary words to communicate with each other.

- Provide feedback throughout the lesson to help students monitor and improve their language use. For example, you might correct errors in pronunciation or grammar during the speaking activity, or provide written feedback on the writing prompts.
- Use the useful phrases and idioms provided in the book to help students communicate more fluently and naturally.
- Use the example classroom activity provided for each theme as a starting point, but feel free to modify and adapt the activity to better suit your students' needs and abilities.
- Encourage students to practice using the new vocabulary and language structures outside of the classroom, such as through homework assignments or self-study activities.
- Finally, assess your students' progress and adjust your teaching approach as needed to help them continue to grow and develop their language skills.

By following these steps and utilizing the resources provided in the book, ESL/EFL teachers can design effective lessons that incorporate principles from Krashen, Swain, Ellis, and Gass to help their students achieve their language learning goals.

Targeted Vocabulary

One of the key aspects of language learning is building a strong vocabulary. In the vocabulary section of this book, you will find 50 targeted vocabulary words for each of the ten themes: Technology, Culture, Environment, Health, Education, Jobs and Careers, Social Issues, Entertainment, Travel, and Relationships. These carefully selected words are chosen to be meaningful not only to the students, but also to the specific theme, allowing for a more relevant and engaging learning experience.

Importance of Targeted Vocabulary:

The vocabulary words in this book have been carefully selected to align with the themes that are relevant to intermediate language learners. This means that the words in the book are not just randomly chosen, but rather they are chosen with a specific purpose in mind. The themes that are relevant to intermediate learners typically include topics such as everyday life, work, travel, entertainment, and culture. By learning vocabulary that is associated with these themes, learners can develop a more nuanced understanding of the language and how it is used in different contexts. Targeted vocabulary is critical for language learners because it enables them to express themselves more effectively and fluently in real-life situations. When learners have a wide range of vocabulary at their disposal, they are able to communicate their ideas more precisely and with greater accuracy. They are also better equipped to understand and respond to what others are saying to them. This is especially important in real-life situations where communication is key, such as in the workplace, at school, or in social settings.

When learners are exposed to vocabulary that is relevant to their interests and needs, they can develop their language skills in a more meaningful and purposeful way. This means that they are more likely to engage with the material and see the value in what they are learning. For example, if a learner is interested in cooking, learning cooking-related vocabulary words can help them communicate about their favorite recipes and cooking techniques. If a learner is preparing for a job interview, learning vocabulary related to the job position and industry can help them communicate more effectively with potential employers.

Incorporating targeted vocabulary into language

lessons can also help students make connections between the language they are learning and the world around them. This can enhance their motivation and engagement in the learning process because they can see how the language is relevant to their own lives. For example, learning vocabulary related to current events or cultural traditions can help learners understand the world around them and develop a greater appreciation for other cultures.

Ways to Make Learning Vocabulary Easy:

As an ESL/EFL teacher, you play a vital role in helping your students learn vocabulary effectively. Here are some strategies that you can use to make learning vocabulary easy for your students:

- **Contextualize Vocabulary**: Introduce new vocabulary words in the context of the themes presented in this book. Use visual aids, real-life examples, and authentic materials to help students understand the meaning and usage of the words in context. This will enable students to connect the words to their prior knowledge and make meaningful associations, making the vocabulary more memorable.

- **Practice in Meaningful Ways**: Provide opportunities for students to practice vocabulary words in meaningful and authentic ways. Incorporate speaking, listening, reading, and writing activities that allow students to actively use the words in communicative tasks. Encourage students to use the words in context, such as in conversations, role-plays, or writing prompts, to reinforce their understanding and retention of the words.

- **Review and Reinforce**: Regularly review and reinforce the targeted vocabulary through various activities and games. Use flashcards, quizzes, word puzzles, or other interactive activities to engage students in reviewing and practicing the words. Provide feedback and corrections as needed and encourage students to self-assess their progress.

- **Personalize Learning**: Encourage students to make the vocabulary words relevant to their own lives by using them in their own sentences, stories, or discussions. This will help students to internalize the words and make them part of their active vocabulary. Encourage students to use vocabulary words in their speaking and writing tasks outside of the classroom as well, to further reinforce their learning.

By utilizing these strategies and activities, teachers can help their students develop a strong vocabulary that is relevant to the themes being taught in "ESL/EFL Instruction for Intermediate Learners: Themed Vocabulary, Speaking, and Writing." This targeted approach to vocabulary instruction makes learning more meaningful and effective, allowing students to apply their newly acquired vocabulary to real-life situations and contexts. With a rich vocabulary, students will be better equipped to communicate effectively in English and achieve success in their language learning journey.

In addition to the strategies mentioned earlier, another effective approach for teaching vocabulary to ESL/EFL learners is based on the research and work of Paul Nation, a renowned linguist and expert in vocabulary acquisition. Nation's research emphasizes the importance of extensive vocabulary exposure and deliberate vocabulary study for language learners.

One key concept from Paul Nation's work is the "4/14/4000" rule, which suggests that learners need to encounter a word at least 4 times in context, study it deliberately at least 14 times, and use it actively in their productive skills (speaking and writing) at least 4000 times in order to fully acquire it. This highlights the need for repeated exposure to vocabulary words in various contexts and using them actively in communication. Here are some ways teachers can incorporate Paul Nation's vocabulary study principles into their instruction:

- **Provide extensive reading opportunities**: Encourage your students to read extensively in English, both inside and outside the classroom. Offer a variety of reading materials, such as graded readers, newspapers, magazines, and online articles, that cover different themes, including the ones in the book's vocabulary section. This will expose students to new vocabulary in context and help reinforce their understanding of the words.

- **Teach high-frequency words**: Paul Nation's research suggests that there are certain high-frequency words that are crucial for learners to acquire in order to communicate effectively in English. These words, often referred to as "core vocabulary," include common nouns, verbs, adjectives, and adverbs that are frequently used in everyday communication. Make sure to include these high-frequency words in your vocabulary instruction and provide ample opportunities for students to practice using them in context.

- **Use deliberate vocabulary study techniques:** Encourage students to engage in deliberate vocabulary study, which involves actively and consciously learning new words. This can include techniques such as creating vocabulary flashcards with the word, definition, and example sentence, using vocabulary notebooks to record new words and their usage, and practicing word formation exercises, such as prefix and suffix activities, to expand word knowledge. Encourage students to review their vocabulary regularly and quiz themselves to reinforce retention.

- **Integrate vocabulary into speaking and writing activities:** Provide opportunities for students to use the vocabulary words actively in speaking and writing activities. For example, in speaking activities, have students engage in discussions, debates, role-plays, and presentations that require them to use the vocabulary words in meaningful ways. In writing activities, encourage students to incorporate the vocabulary words into essays, paragraphs, and other written assignments. This will help students practice using the words in context and reinforce their understanding and retention of the vocabulary.

- **Offer differentiated instruction:** Recognize that students have different levels of vocabulary proficiency and offer differentiated instruction to meet their needs. Some students may need more practice with basic vocabulary words, while others may be ready for more advanced vocabulary. Provide additional support or challenge as needed and scaffold instruction accordingly.

Incorporating Paul Nation's research-based principles of vocabulary study can greatly enhance the effectiveness of your vocabulary instruction and help students develop a rich and diverse vocabulary repertoire that is relevant to the themes covered in the book. By providing extensive exposure to vocabulary in context, using deliberate vocabulary study techniques, integrating vocabulary into speaking and writing activities, and offering differentiated instruction, you can empower your students to become more confident and proficient English language learners. Overall, the combination of targeted vocabulary words based on themes and Paul Nation's vocabulary study principles can provide a comprehensive and effective approach to vocabulary instruction for intermediate ESL/EFL learners.

Here are some examples of activities that can be used to target vocabulary for intermediate English language learners (ESL/EFL):

- **Vocabulary flashcards**: Create flashcards with new vocabulary words and their definitions. Students can review them individually or with a partner. For added practice, have students create their own flashcards.
- **Word games**: Play games like Scrabble or Bananagrams to practice vocabulary. Students can also create their own word games such as crossword puzzles or word searches using their new vocabulary words.
- **Word webs**: Have students create word webs or mind maps with new vocabulary words. They can connect the words to related concepts, synonyms, or antonyms.

- **Role-playing**: Use new vocabulary words in role-playing scenarios. For example, students can act out a job interview or a doctor's visit using new medical vocabulary.
- **Reading and writing**: Assign reading materials that include new vocabulary words. Have students underline or highlight the new words, then use them in writing assignments.
- **Vocabulary journal**: Ask students to keep a vocabulary journal where they record new words, their definitions, and example sentences. They can also include pictures or drawings to help them remember the words.
- **Vocabulary quizzes**: Create quizzes to test students' knowledge of new vocabulary words. This can be done using online tools or on paper.
- **Vocabulary debates**: Have students debate a topic using their new vocabulary words. This can be done in pairs or small groups.
- **Vocabulary word of the day**: Introduce a new vocabulary word each day and have students use it in conversation or writing assignments.

Speaking Prompts

Speaking prompts are a crucial tool for English language learners and using speaking prompts in the classroom has several benefits for language learners. Firstly, they provide learners with a structured and supported way to practice speaking skills. This can be particularly important for learners who may feel shy or lacking in confidence when it comes to speaking in English. The prompts provide a clear starting point and allow learners to build their skills gradually.

Secondly, speaking prompts allow learners to apply newly acquired vocabulary and grammatical structures in a practical and meaningful way. This can help to reinforce their learning and make it more memorable. The themed organization of the prompts in "ESL/EFL Instruction for Intermediate Learners" helps learners to make connections between different aspects of language and to see how vocabulary and structures are used in context. Finally, speaking prompts provide learners with opportunities to receive feedback on their language use. This can be particularly valuable in identifying areas where learners may need additional support or practice. Feedback can be provided by a teacher or by peers, and can help learners to develop their skills over time.

In "ESL/EFL Instruction for Intermediate Learners: Themed Vocabulary, Speaking, and Writing," the speaking prompts are organized into 10 themes: Technology, Culture, Environment, Health, Education, Jobs and Careers, Social Issues, Entertainment, Travel, and Relationships. This organization allows learners to engage with topics that are relevant to their lives and interests, which can help to keep them motivated and engaged in the learning process.

The use of speaking prompts is grounded in the work of language acquisition theorists Stephen Krashen and Merrill Swain. Krashen's input hypothesis, which was explained earlier, suggests that language learners acquire language through exposure to input that is slightly beyond their current level of language proficiency. When learners are presented with speaking prompts, they are provided with prompts that require them to use new vocabulary or grammatical structures, providing them with input that is slightly beyond their current level. This can help them to acquire language more effectively, as they are being exposed to language that is just challenging enough to push them to develop their language skills, but not so challenging that they become overwhelmed and unable to understand the input. The use of prompts also allows learners to engage with language in a meaningful way, as they are encouraged to use the language to express their ideas and thoughts on a given topic.

Additionally, Krashen's affective filter hypothesis suggests that learners need to be motivated and have a positive attitude in order to acquire language effectively. Using speaking prompts that are relevant and interesting to learners, as is the case in "ESL/EFL Instruction for Intermediate Learners: Themed Vocabulary, Speaking, and Writing," can help to keep learners engaged and motivated in the learning process. This, in turn, can help to lower the affective filter, allowing learners to be more receptive to the input and thus acquire language more effectively.

Merrill Swain is a Canadian applied linguist who has made significant contributions to our understanding of second language acquisition. Her Output Hypothesis states that language learners need opportunities to produce language in order to improve their proficiency. According to Swain, learners need to be engaged in meaningful communication and actively produce language, rather than simply receiving input passively. In this way, learners have to "work through" their language gaps and errors to produce meaningful language output, which then allows them to notice and address the gaps in their language knowledge.

Speaking prompts can be a powerful tool in implementing Swain's Output Hypothesis in the classroom. By using speaking prompts, teachers can provide learners with opportunities to produce language and engage in meaningful communication. As learners work through the prompts, they are challenged to express their ideas using new vocabulary, grammatical structures, and discourse functions. In this way, they are able to practice and refine their language skills.

Furthermore, when learners engage with speaking prompts, they receive feedback on their language production from their teachers or peers, which can help them identify areas where they need to improve. This feedback can also help learners recognize and fix errors in their language production. By providing opportunities for learners to produce language, engage in meaningful communication, and receive feedback, speaking prompts can facilitate language learning and support the development of learners' proficiency in the target language.

Overall, the use of speaking prompts in second language acquisition is related to Krashen's and Swain's research in that it provides learners with opportunities to produce meaningful output and be exposed to meaningful input. It also helps keep learners motivated and engaged in the learning process.

Here are a few examples of speaking prompt activities that follow the comprehensible input and comprehensible output hypotheses:

Comprehensible Input:

- **Picture descriptions**: Students are given a picture and asked to describe it in detail, using newly acquired vocabulary and grammar structures. The teacher can scaffold the activity by providing sentence starters or word banks to help students construct their sentences.
- **Story retelling**: Students listen to or read a short story and are then asked to retell it in their own words. The teacher can provide comprehension questions or prompts to guide the retelling and

ensure that students are using new vocabulary and grammar structures in their responses.

- **Information gap activities**: Students are given incomplete information and must ask their partner questions to fill in the gaps. For example, one student might have a picture of a city and the other student might have a list of attractions to visit. They must ask each other questions to plan a day of sightseeing in the city.

Comprehensible Output:

- **Role plays**: Students are given a scenario and must act it out using newly acquired vocabulary and grammar structures. For example, students might role-play a job interview, a doctor's appointment, or a customer service interaction. The teacher can provide prompts or sentence starters to help guide the conversation.
- **Debate or discussion**: Students are given a controversial topic and must argue for or against it, using newly acquired vocabulary and grammar structures. The teacher can provide sentence frames or argumentative language to help scaffold the discussion.

- **Interview**: Students are paired up and must interview each other using newly acquired vocabulary and grammar structures. For example, they might ask about each other's hobbies, interests, or goals. The teacher can provide prompts or sentence starters to help guide the conversation.

These activities provide opportunities for students to receive comprehensible input or produce comprehensible output in a structured and supportive environment, helping to facilitate second language acquisition.

Useful Phrases

Learning a language is not only about learning individual words but also about understanding how words are used in context. This is where useful phrases come in. Useful phrases are groups of words that are commonly used together to express a particular idea or convey a certain message. By teaching useful phrases, teachers can provide learners with the tools they need to communicate effectively in various contexts.

In this book, twenty useful phrases have been compiled for each of the ten themes: technology, culture, environment, health, education, jobs and careers, social issues, entertainment, travel, and relationships. These phrases are carefully selected to reflect common situations and scenarios that learners may encounter in their daily lives. By learning these phrases, learners can better understand how the language is used in context and apply them in their own conversations and writing assignments.

One important aspect of teaching useful phrases is to provide learners with exposure to the language as it is used in context. This means that teachers need to show learners not only how the phrases are used but also the situations in which they are used. For example, when teaching the theme of travel, teachers can show learners how to use phrases such as " How do I get to [attraction] from here?" or " Do I need to get a visa to travel to [destination]?" in real-life situations. This helps learners to understand how the language is used in context and increases their confidence in using the phrases themselves.

Another effective method of teaching useful phrases is to incorporate them into lessons and activities. For example, the phrases can be used as examples during presentations or discussions, encouraging learners to use them in their writing assignments and conversations. Exercises can also be created that give learners opportunities to practice using the phrases in dialogues, role-plays, and other interactive activities. This allows learners to practice the phrases in a supportive and controlled environment, increasing their chances of using them effectively in real-life situations.

Merrill Swain's output hypothesis and Rod Ellis and Susan Gass's interaction method (task-based language learning) are two influential theories in the field of language learning that highlight the importance of teaching useful phrases to language learners. Swain's output hypothesis proposes that learners need to engage in meaningful output production in order to develop their language proficiency. This hypothesis argues that through the process of producing language, learners are able to reflect on the rules and structures of the language, and they can make the necessary adjustments to improve their fluency and accuracy. Therefore, by teaching learners useful phrases, teachers are providing them with the opportunity to produce more language and develop their proficiency.

In addition, the interaction method developed by Rod Ellis and Susan Gass emphasizes the importance of communication and interaction in language learning. This method advocates for task-based language learning, which involves learners in communicative activities that require them to use the language in context. By incorporating useful phrases into task-based activities, learners are provided with opportunities to interact with the language and use it in meaningful ways. This not only helps learners to develop their communicative competence, but it also allows them to acquire useful language that they can use in real-life situations.

Furthermore, by teaching useful phrases, teachers can

help learners to build their confidence and motivation in language learning. Learners may feel more comfortable and successful when they are able to use the language in authentic situations, and they may be more motivated to continue learning if they feel that they are making progress and able to communicate effectively. By learning and using useful phrases, learners are able to produce more language and develop their fluency and accuracy.

Here are some examples of how teachers can incorporate useful phrases into ESL/EFL lessons:

- **Role-plays**: Teachers can create role-plays that require students to use the useful phrases related to the lesson topic. For example, if the lesson is about travel, teachers can create a role-play where students practice using phrases such as "I would like to book a ticket to Paris" or "Can you recommend a good restaurant?"
- **Vocabulary activities**: Teachers can use vocabulary activities such as matching or fill-in-the-blank exercises that require students to use the useful phrases in context. For example, if the lesson is about social issues, teachers can provide students

with a list of useful phrases such as "I disagree with your opinion because..." and ask them to match the phrases with their definitions.

- **Group discussions**: Teachers can facilitate group discussions that require students to use the useful phrases to express their opinions and ideas. For example, if the lesson is about culture, teachers can divide students into groups and ask them to discuss their favorite cultural traditions using phrases such as "In my culture, we celebrate by..." or "I think cultural traditions are important because..."

- **Writing activities**: Teachers can assign writing activities that require students to use the useful phrases in written form. For example, if the lesson is about jobs and careers, teachers can ask students to write a job application letter using phrases such as "I am writing to apply for the position of..." or "I believe I would be a good fit for this job because..."

- **Listening activities**: Teachers can use listening activities that incorporate the useful phrases into the audio or video materials. For example, if the lesson is about technology, teachers can provide students with a listening activity where they have to listen to a podcast or a video about the latest technology trends and identify the useful phrases used by the speakers.

By incorporating useful phrases into these types of activities, teachers can provide students with the opportunity to practice using the language in context, which can help them to develop their communicative competence and fluency in the language.

Writing Prompts

Writing is a fundamental skill in language acquisition and a critical component of second language learning. The ability to express oneself in writing is necessary for learners to communicate their ideas and thoughts in a clear and organized manner. This is why writing prompts are essential tools for teachers to help their students develop their writing skills.

In this book, there are three writing prompts for each of the ten themes, providing learners with a diverse range of topics to write about. These prompts are relevant to learners' interests and experiences, and they are intended to ignite their creativity and engage them in the writing process. Moreover, these prompts are designed to provide structure to learners who may struggle with organizing their thoughts or expressing themselves in writing.

Writing prompts help learners develop their critical thinking and creative skills as they force learners to think deeply about a given topic and generate new ideas and perspectives. Additionally, they provide learners with an opportunity to practice their language skills in a meaningful and authentic way. By writing about topics that are relevant to their lives and experiences, learners are more likely to be motivated and engaged in the writing process.

To teach writing prompts and writing effectively, teachers can provide clear instructions and expectations for the writing assignment, as well as model the writing process for their students. Teachers can also provide feedback and corrections on the students' writing, helping them improve their grammar, vocabulary, and sentence structure. Through these methods, teachers can guide learners towards becoming better writers.

Research supports the effectiveness of using writing prompts in second language acquisition. James Britton, an influential language educator, argued that writing is not just a tool for communication but also a means for learning. In his view, writing allows learners to explore and construct their own knowledge, which in turn promotes language development.

Britton's research highlights the importance of the writing process and how it can facilitate language acquisition. He emphasized that writing is not just about producing a final product, but also about the process of generating ideas, organizing thoughts, and revising and editing.

In the context of second language acquisition, Britton's research is particularly relevant as it suggests that writing can be a powerful tool for language learners. By engaging in the writing process, learners are able to practice their language skills in a meaningful and authentic way. Writing prompts can provide learners with opportunities to use the language they are learning in a purposeful context, and to receive feedback on their language use.

Moreover, Britton's work emphasizes the importance of scaffolding in the writing process. Teachers can support their students by providing them with guidance, feedback, and support throughout the writing process. This can include providing models of good writing, giving feedback on drafts, and providing opportunities for peer review and collaboration.

Swain's Output Hypothesis has significant implications for writing instruction in language acquisition as well. Writing provides learners with an opportunity to produce output in a structured and organized way. Through writing, learners can practice producing output in a low-stakes environment where they can take their time to organize their thoughts and express themselves clearly.

Swain also emphasizes the importance of feedback in the language learning process. Writing provides a platform for feedback, where learners can receive corrective feedback on their written output. This feedback helps learners to identify areas where they need improvement and make the necessary changes to improve their language skills.

Research has shown that Swain's Output Hypothesis is supported by empirical evidence. A study by Sauro and Smith found that learners who produced more language output had greater improvements in their language skills than those who only received input. Writing is an effective tool for producing language output and receiving feedback on that output, making it a valuable tool in second language acquisition.

Here are some examples of activities that ESL/EFL teachers can use to incorporate writing prompts into their lessons:

- **Journal Writing**: Students can write daily journal entries based on a writing prompt related to the theme they are studying. This activity can be done individually or in pairs, and can be used as a warm-up activity at the beginning of class or as a homework assignment.

- **Peer Feedback**: After students complete a writing assignment based on a prompt, they can exchange papers with a partner and provide feedback on each other's writing. This can help students to develop their editing and revision skills, as well as provide them with an opportunity to practice giving and receiving feedback.

- **Creative Writing**: Teachers can provide students with a writing prompt that encourages them to use their imaginations and creativity. For example, students could be asked to write a short story or poem based on a given prompt.

- **Research Writing**: Students can be given a writing prompt that requires them to conduct research on a topic related to the theme they are studying. This can help students to develop their research skills and deepen their understanding of the topic.

- **Debate Writing**: Students can be given a writing prompt that requires them to take a position on a controversial topic related to the theme they are studying. They can then write a persuasive essay arguing for their position.

- **Collaborative Writing**: Students can work in pairs or small groups to write a story, report, or other type of document based on a given writing prompt. This activity can help students to develop their collaboration and teamwork skills, as well as their writing skills.

These are just a few examples of the many ways in which ESL/EFL teachers can use writing prompts to enhance their students' writing skills and promote second language acquisition.

Fun Idioms & Phrases

Learning idioms is an essential part of mastering a new language, as it helps language learners to understand and communicate more effectively with native speakers. In this book, there are several fun idioms and phrases for each of the ten themes, providing learners with a variety of expressions to use in their speaking and writing.

Idioms are important for language learners for several reasons. One reason is that idioms provide learners with a deeper understanding of the culture and context of the target language. Many idioms are rooted in the history and traditions of the language and learning them can help learners to connect more authentically with native speakers.

Another benefit is that idioms help learners to sound more natural and fluent in the target language. Native speakers often use idioms in their everyday speech and incorporating them into one's own speech can help to improve fluency and accuracy. Idioms also add color and personality to one's language use, making it more interesting and engaging.

Idioms also challenge learners to think creatively and

critically about language use. Idioms often have metaphorical meanings that are not immediately obvious, requiring learners to use their analytical skills to decipher their meanings. This can help learners to develop their critical thinking skills and improve their ability to understand and use figurative language.

The significance of idioms in second language acquisition is supported by research, which has indicated that learning idiomatic expressions can be an effective way to improve language skills. One theoretical framework that supports this approach is the Lexical Approach. The Lexical Approach emphasizes the importance of learning vocabulary in context and in phrases or chunks, rather than as isolated words. This approach is based on the idea that language learners need to develop a large "lexical repertoire" of words and phrases in order to achieve fluency and communicate effectively in the target language.

According to Michael Lewis, who introduced the Lexical Approach in 1993, idioms are an important part of this lexical repertoire. Idioms are fixed expressions that have a specific meaning that cannot be easily deduced from the literal meaning of the words. For example, "to hit the nail on the head" means to be exactly right about something, but the literal meaning of the words doesn't convey this idea.

To effectively teach idioms in class, teachers can provide contextualized examples of idiomatic expressions and encourage students to use them in conversation and writing activities. Visual aids, such as images or videos, can also be used to help students understand the meaning and context of idioms.

Teachers can also incorporate fun activities and games to help learners remember and use idioms in context. For example, teachers can ask learners to create a story or dialogue using idioms, or have learners play a game where they guess the meaning of idioms based on their context.

Here are some examples of activities that can help ESL/EFL teachers teach idioms:

- **Idiom guessing game**: In this activity, the teacher writes several idioms on slips of paper and puts them in a hat. One student comes up and picks a slip of paper, reads the idiom to the class, and asks them to guess what it means. The class can discuss and come up with possible meanings together.

- **Idiom matching game**: The teacher provides a list of idioms and their meanings. The students must match the idiom to the correct meaning.
- **Idiom role-play**: The teacher assigns pairs of students different idioms to act out in a short skit. The rest of the class must guess which idiom is being acted out.
- **Idiom storytelling**: The teacher provides the students with a list of idioms and asks them to incorporate as many of the idioms into a short story as they can.
- **Idiom fill-in-the-blank**: The teacher provides a story or sentence with idioms missing. The students must fill in the blanks with the correct idioms.
- **Idiom flashcards**: The teacher provides the students with a set of idiom flashcards, with the idiom on one side and the meaning on the other. The students can quiz each other on the meanings of the idioms.
- **Idiom charades:** The teacher assigns a group of students an idiom to act out silently while the rest of the class tries to guess what the idiom is.

These activities can be adapted and modified to fit the needs and language level of the students. By incorporating idioms into their lessons and providing opportunities for students to practice using them, teachers can help their students develop a more natural and fluent communication style in the target language.

Classroom Activity

Classroom activities are an essential part of ESL/EFL instruction, as they provide language learners with opportunities to practice their language skills in an engaging and interactive way. By using classroom activities, teachers can create an immersive learning environment that promotes active participation and collaboration among students.

Research has shown that classroom activities can be highly effective in improving language acquisition. For example, a study by Nunan and Lamb found that students who engaged in collaborative activities such as group discussions and role-plays showed significant improvement in their language proficiency compared to those who only received traditional classroom instruction.

One important aspect of using classroom activities effectively is to ensure that the learning objectives and expectations are clearly communicated to students. Teachers should explain to their students why they are doing a particular activity and what they can expect to gain from it. This helps students to stay motivated and focused, as they understand the purpose and relevance of the activity to their language learning goals.

In addition, teachers should also encourage students to reflect on their learning after completing a classroom activity. Reflection helps students to consolidate their understanding and identify areas for improvement. By providing constructive feedback and guidance, teachers can help their students to further develop their language skills.

The classroom activities included in each of the ten themes in this book are meant to serve as examples and inspiration for ESL/EFL teachers. While these activities have been carefully crafted to align with the content and language objectives of each theme, teachers are encouraged to use these activities as a starting point and tailor them to meet the specific needs of their students.

In addition to the provided activities, teachers can also use the themes and vocabulary lists as a basis for creating their own classroom lessons and activities. For example, the technology theme includes vocabulary related to computers, smartphones, and social media. Teachers can use this vocabulary to create activities such as online research projects, social media debates, or writing prompts about the benefits and drawbacks of technology.

The key is to design activities that are engaging, relevant, and appropriate for the language proficiency level of the students. By using the themes and vocabulary lists as a guide, and the example classroom activities as a jumping off point, teachers can create activities that are not only language-focused but also content-driven, providing students with a well-rounded learning experience.

Overall, the provided classroom activities and themes are meant to be flexible and adaptable, allowing teachers to use them in a way that best suits their teaching style and the needs of their students. By using these resources as a starting point, teachers can create dynamic and effective language lessons that engage students and facilitate second language acquisition.

Here are some tips for creating effective classroom activities for ESL/EFL learners:

- Identify clear learning objectives: Before designing an activity, it is important to identify what you want your students to learn or achieve. This will help you choose appropriate activities and guide your planning.

- Consider learners' interests and experiences: Choose activities that are relevant to your learners' interests and experiences. This will make the activities more engaging and help learners connect the language to their own lives.
- Balance challenge and support: Activities should provide enough challenge to keep learners engaged and motivated, but not so much that they become frustrated. Be sure to provide support, such as clear instructions and appropriate feedback.
- Use a variety of activities: Different learners have different strengths and preferences, so it's important to use a variety of activities to cater to these differences. This can also help keep learners engaged and motivated.
- Incorporate authentic materials: Using real-world materials, such as news articles, videos, or advertisements, can help learners develop their language skills in a more authentic context.
- Encourage collaboration and interaction: Many ESL/EFL learners come from cultures where collaboration is not emphasized in learning. Encourage interaction among learners and with the teacher in activities, as this can help learners

practice their language skills in a more natural way.

- Be flexible: Be prepared to modify activities based on learners' needs and interests, and be open to feedback from learners about what works and what doesn't.

By following these tips, teachers can create effective and engaging classroom activities that help their ESL/EFL learners develop their language skills in a meaningful way.

Action Research

Action research is a type of research that emphasizes the active participation of teachers in developing their own classroom practices, with the goal of improving student learning outcomes. In the context of second language acquisition, action research can be a valuable tool for teachers to evaluate the effectiveness of their instructional practices and to make evidence-based decisions about how to improve them.

In this book, a notes section is included at the end of each theme, which can be used for action research purposes. These notes provide a space for teachers to reflect on their teaching practices and to document their observations of student learning during classroom activities related to the theme.

Research has shown that action research can have a positive impact on both teachers and students. For example, a study by Burns and Richards found that ESL teachers who engaged in action research reported increased confidence in their teaching abilities and a greater sense of empowerment in their professional roles. Additionally, students of teachers who engaged in action research showed improvements in their language proficiency, as well as their motivation and engagement in the classroom.

To conduct action research effectively, teachers should follow a structured process that includes identifying a research question or problem, collecting and analyzing data, and making changes to their teaching practices based on the findings. Teachers can use a variety of data collection methods, such as classroom observations, student interviews or surveys, and analysis of student work samples.

By conducting action research, teachers can gain a deeper understanding of their students' learning needs and develop more effective instructional practices. The notes section in each theme of this book provides a starting point for teachers to engage in action research and improve their teaching practices, ultimately leading to better outcomes for their students.

Here are some steps for conducting action research in second language teaching:

- **Identify a research question**: The first step in conducting action research is to identify a research question or area of inquiry. This question should be focused and specific, and should address an area of teaching or learning that you want to improve. For example, a research question might be: "How can I improve my students' speaking fluency in English?"

- **Collect data**: Once you have identified your research question, you will need to collect data to help you answer it. This might involve collecting data from your students through surveys, interviews, or assessments. You might also collect data on your own teaching practices through self-reflection, classroom observations, or peer evaluations.

- **Analyze the data**: Once you have collected your data, you will need to analyze it to draw conclusions about your research question. This might involve looking for patterns in your students' performance or identifying areas where your teaching practices could be improved.

- **Develop an action plan**: Based on your analysis of the data, you should develop an action plan for making changes to your teaching practices. This might involve trying out new teaching strategies, using different materials, or adjusting your lesson plans.

- **Implement the changes**: Once you have developed your action plan, you should implement the changes in your classroom. This might involve trying out new teaching strategies or materials, or making adjustments to your lesson plans.

- **Collect data on the impact of the changes**: After you have implemented the changes, you should collect data on their impact. This might involve administering assessments or surveys to your students to see if their performance has improved, or reflecting on your own teaching practices to see if you are more effective.

- **Reflect on the process**: Finally, you should reflect on the action research process itself. This might involve asking yourself questions like: What did I learn from this process? What worked well and what could be improved? What would I do differently next time?

For example, let's say a teacher's research question is "How can I improve my students' speaking fluency in English?" They might collect data by conducting pre-

and post-assessments on their students' speaking fluency, observing their own teaching practices, and interviewing students to get their feedback on the effectiveness of different teaching strategies. Based on their analysis of the data, they might develop an action plan that includes using more authentic materials, providing more opportunities for speaking practice, and incorporating peer feedback into the classroom. They would then implement these changes in their classroom and collect data on their impact by conducting post-assessments and continuing to observe their own teaching practices. Finally, they would reflect on the process and make adjustments as needed for future action research projects.

Assessments

Assessing students' language proficiency is an essential component of effective ESL/EFL instruction. Proper assessment helps teachers determine students' level of language acquisition, which in turn informs lesson planning and allows for targeted instruction to meet students' needs. It is important for teachers to differentiate between beginner, intermediate, and advanced levels of language proficiency to properly assess their students.

There are several methods that teachers can use to assess their students' language proficiency. One commonly used method is the Common European Framework of Reference for Languages (CEFR), which divides language proficiency into six levels ranging from A1 (beginner) to C2 (advanced). Another method is the Language Proficiency Assessment (LPA), which assesses students' abilities in reading, writing, listening, and speaking. Additionally, teachers can use informal assessments, such as observations and student self-assessments, to supplement formal assessments.

It is important for teachers to properly administer assessments to ensure accurate results. This includes providing clear instructions and directions, creating a comfortable testing environment, and using reliable and valid assessment tools. Teachers should also consider the cultural and linguistic backgrounds of their students and ensure that assessments are culturally sensitive and appropriate.

Research has shown that effective assessment practices can lead to improved student outcomes. For example, a study by Shohamy and Inbar found that using a combination of assessment methods, including self-assessment and peer assessment, helped promote learner autonomy and increased motivation among language learners. Similarly, a study by Brown and Hudson found that using multiple assessment methods allowed for a more comprehensive understanding of students' language proficiency and better informed instructional practices.

Informal Assessments

Informal assessment is an ongoing process in which teachers gather information about their students' language proficiency levels in a less structured way than formal assessments. This type of assessment is often used to monitor progress, provide feedback, and adjust instruction accordingly. Here are some ways that teachers can informally assess their students' levels:

- Classroom observation: Teachers can observe their students' language use during classroom activities, discussions, and group work. They can pay attention to the vocabulary, grammar, and fluency levels of their students and use this information to inform their instruction.

- Conversations: Teachers can engage in one-on-one conversations with their students to assess their speaking and listening skills. They can ask open-ended questions, listen for pronunciation and intonation, and assess their ability to understand and respond appropriately.

- Writing assignments: Teachers can assign writing tasks such as journal entries, short essays, or summaries, and use these as a way to assess their students' writing proficiency. They can look for errors in grammar, spelling, and sentence structure, as well as assess the clarity and coherence of their writing.

- Self-assessment: Teachers can ask their students to self-assess their language proficiency levels using a rubric or checklist. This can help students reflect on their own strengths and weaknesses and identify areas for improvement.

Research has shown that informal assessments can be just as effective as formal assessments in providing information about students' language proficiency levels. Using a combination of informal and formal assessments can help teachers gain a more comprehensive understanding of their students' language abilities and tailor instruction to meet their needs.

Assessment in the Classroom

Assessing students' language proficiency is an essential part of any ESL/EFL classroom. There are various ways to assess students' work in different language domains, including speaking, reading, listening, and writing. In addition, teachers can use both formative and summative assessments to evaluate their students' progress throughout the semester.

Formative assessments are evaluations that occur throughout the learning process, and they are designed to help teachers identify their students' strengths and weaknesses. These assessments can help teachers adjust their instruction to better meet students' needs.

Examples of formative assessments in an ESL/EFL classroom could include:

- **In-class discussions**: During discussions, teachers can observe students' language proficiency in speaking and listening and provide feedback on areas that need improvement.
- **Peer review**: Students can provide feedback on each other's writing or speaking assignments, helping identify areas that need improvement.
- **Quizzes**: Short quizzes can be used to assess students' understanding of specific language topics.

Summative assessments are evaluations that occur at the end of a learning period and are used to evaluate a student's overall proficiency level. These assessments are typically used to assign grades or determine if a student has met certain language proficiency standards. Examples of summative assessments in an ESL/EFL classroom could include:

- **Standardized tests**: Many ESL/EFL programs require students to take standardized tests, such as the TOEFL or IELTS, to demonstrate their language proficiency.
- **Final exams**: Final exams can assess students' proficiency in all language domains, including

reading, writing, speaking, and listening.

- **Essays**: Writing assignments can be used to evaluate students' ability to use grammar and vocabulary appropriately in written communication.

To properly conduct both formative and summative assessments, ESL/EFL teachers can follow these steps:

- **Identify the language domains and skills to be assessed**: Teachers should select assessments that align with their learning objectives and student needs.

- **Choose appropriate assessment tools**: Teachers should choose assessments that are reliable, valid, and fair to all students. For example, if assessing reading comprehension, teachers might choose a reading passage followed by comprehension questions.

- **Administer the assessment**: Teachers should provide clear instructions to students before administering the assessment and ensure that the testing environment is conducive to learning.

- **Evaluate student work**: Teachers should carefully review and grade student work, providing feedback on areas that need improvement.

- **Use the assessment results:** Teachers can use the results of assessments to adjust their instruction to better meet students' needs, provide feedback to students on areas that need improvement, and assign grades or determine if students have met certain proficiency standards.

Research has shown that both formative and summative assessments are important for evaluating students' language proficiency and improving language instruction. For example, a study by Black and Wiliam found that using formative assessments improved student achievement and motivation in various subject areas. Similarly, a study by McFarlane and Sakui found that summative assessments helped ESL/EFL teachers identify students' strengths and weaknesses and provided a basis for adjusting instruction to better meet students' needs.

Lesson Plan

A lesson plan is a crucial tool for ESL/EFL teachers as they provide a clear structure and direction for each lesson. By creating a well-planned lesson, teachers can ensure that their students are engaged, challenged, and making progress towards their language learning goals. One of the primary benefits of having a lesson plan is that it helps teachers to be more organized and efficient with their time. With a clear plan in place, teachers can minimize the risk of running out of time, missing key objectives, or failing to adequately cover important topics. A well-prepared lesson plan also helps teachers to anticipate and prepare for potential challenges that may arise during the lesson, such as difficulties with student comprehension or disruptions in the classroom. This can save time and reduce stress during the lesson itself. Additionally, a lesson plan allows teachers to identify and prepare any necessary materials in advance, such as worksheets, activities, or audiovisual aids.

Another key benefit of a lesson plan is that it helps to ensure that lessons are aligned with the needs and abilities of the students. By taking into account the students' level of proficiency, learning style, and individual needs, teachers can design lessons that are both challenging and attainable. This helps to keep students motivated and engaged in the learning process.

Lesson plans also provide a clear framework for assessment and evaluation. By defining clear objectives, teachers can assess whether or not their students have achieved the intended learning outcomes. This information can then be used to modify future lessons or adjust teaching methods as needed. In addition, lesson plans also provide a record of what has been taught and can be used for future reference or to track student progress. This can be especially useful when teaching a course over an extended period of time.

In this book, there is a simple lesson plan template included that is designed to assist ESL/EFL teachers in planning their lessons effectively. The template provides a basic structure for planning out a lesson, including sections for objectives, materials needed, activities, and assessment. By using this template, teachers can easily organize their thoughts and ideas, ensuring that they cover all the necessary content and objectives in their lesson.

Date:

☐ Basic   ☐ Intermediate   ☐ Advanced

Lesson Plan

Materials	Objectives

Topic Introduction

Instruction	☐ Reading ☐ Listening
	☐ Writing ☐ Speaking

Production	☐ Reading ☐ Listening
	☐ Writing ☐ Speaking

Practice/Assessment	☐ Reading ☐ Listening
	☐ Writing ☐ Speaking

Intermediate ESL/EFL Prompts

Technology

Targeted Vocabulary:

- Device
- Gadget
- App
- Software
- Hardware
- Operating system
- Interface
- User-friendly
- Upgrade
- Download
- Upload
- Browser
- Internet connection
- Bandwidth
- Firewall
- Antivirus
- Spam
- Phishing
- Hacking
- Encryption
- Cloud computing
- Social media
- Blogging
- Vlogging
- Streaming
- Virtual reality
- Augmented reality
- Artificial intelligence
- Machine learning
- Robotics
- Computer
- Internet
- Keyboard
- Mouse
- Screen
- Monitor
- Printer
- Scanner
- USB drive
- Microphone
- Speaker
- Headphones
- Webcam
- Network
- Email
- Password
- Login
- Website
- Search engine
- Link

Technology

Technology Speaking Prompts:

- What kinds of technology do you use every day?
- How has technology changed your life?
- Do you prefer to read books or e-books? Why?
- What are some benefits and drawbacks of using social media?
- Do you think technology is making people more or less social?
- What do you think is the most important technological innovation of the past 50 years? Why?
- Do you think robots will replace human workers in the future? Why or why not?
- Do you think virtual reality will become more popular in the future? Why or why not?
- What are some ways technology has made the world a better place?
- Do you think people are too dependent on technology? Why or why not?
- What do you think are some of the most important ethical issues surrounding technology?

Technology

Technology Speaking Prompts:

- What are some ways technology has changed the way we communicate?
- Do you think technology has made it easier or more difficult to learn new things? Why?
- How has technology affected the job market in your country?
- What are some ways technology has changed the entertainment industry?
- How has technology impacted the way we travel?
- What do you think are some of the most promising new technologies?
- How has technology affected the environment?
- Do you think technology will eventually lead to the end of privacy? Why or why not?
- What are some ways technology has improved healthcare?

Technology

Useful Phrases:

- I can't seem to connect to the Wi-Fi. Can you help me troubleshoot?
- How has technology changed the way we communicate?
- I think technology can be addictive. What do you think?
- Do you prefer to read physical books or ebooks? Why?
- The Internet has made information more accessible. Do you think this is a good thing?
- Can you recommend any good tech podcasts or YouTube channels?
- I'm not very tech-savvy. Can you recommend a good online course for beginners?
- What are your thoughts on social media? Does it have more benefits or drawbacks?
- What's the most interesting tech innovation you've seen in the past year?
- Can you give me some tips on how to stay safe online?

Technology

Useful Phrases:

- What are some advantages and disadvantages of using virtual reality technology?
- Do you think robots will eventually take over some jobs currently done by humans?
- What are your thoughts on the use of drones in society?
- Have you ever used a smart home device like Amazon Alexa or Google Home? What did you think of it?
- What are your thoughts on the rise of remote work and online learning?
- What do you think about the impact of technology on the environment?
- Do you think video games can be educational? Why or why not?
- Can you recommend any good tech conferences or events?
- How do you think technology will continue to evolve in the next 10 years?
- Can you explain the difference between cloud storage and local storage?

Technology

Writing Prompts:

- Write about a new technology that you would like to try and why. What are the benefits of this technology? How do you think it could change your life?

- Write a review of your favorite website or online game. What do you like about it? What are the features that you find most useful? What improvements would you suggest?

- Write about the role that technology plays in your daily life. How do you use technology to stay connected with others, learn new things, or stay entertained? What are some of the challenges you face when using technology, and how do you overcome them?

Technology

Fun Technology Idioms & Phrases:

- **Out of the loop** - to be uninformed or unaware of the latest news or developments in technology.
- **Plug and play** - refers to technology that is easy to set up and use without requiring technical knowledge or expertise.
- **Crash and burn** - refers to a technology or software that fails or stops working suddenly.
- **Ghost in the machine** - refers to a mysterious technical glitch or malfunction.
- **Technophobe** - someone who is afraid or resistant to new technology.
- **Blue screen of death** - a term used to describe the blue error screen that appears when a Windows computer crashes.
- **Cyberspace** - refers to the virtual world of the internet.
- **Digital footprint** - refers to the trail of personal information and data that is left behind when someone uses the internet or digital devices.

Technology

Fun Technology Idioms & Phrases:

- **Clickbait** - refers to content online that is designed to attract clicks and views, often with sensational or misleading headlines.
- **Going viral** - refers to content that becomes widely popular or shared on the internet.

Technology

Classroom Activity:

- Activity: Tech Talk Debate
- Objectives:
  - To develop critical thinking and communication skills by debating about the advantages and disadvantages of technology.
- Materials:
  - List of debate topics related to technology
  - Timer
- Instructions:
  - Divide the class into two teams (Pro and Con) and provide them with a list of debate topics related to technology. Example topics include:
    - Smartphones should be allowed in classrooms.
    - Social media has more advantages than disadvantages.
    - Online shopping is more convenient than traditional shopping.
    - Technology makes people lazy.
    - The internet should be free for everyone.
  - Each team should choose a topic and prepare their arguments for and against the motion.
  - The teams will then take turns to present their arguments within a set time limit. The team presenting the argument should nominate a speaker to present their views.
  - After each speaker presents their views, the opposing team should have a chance to rebut the argument.

Technology

Classroom Activity:

- Instructions (con't):
    - After all the speakers have presented their arguments, each team should have a chance to summarize their points and make a closing statement.
    - The class can then vote on which team presented the strongest argument and declare a winner.

This activity not only helps students practice their speaking and listening skills but also encourages them to think critically about the advantages and disadvantages of technology.

Notes

Culture

Targeted Vocabulary:

- Tradition
- Customs
- Values
- Beliefs
- Diversity
- Ethnicity
- Heritage
- Multicultural
- Cuisine
- Art
- Music
- Literature
- Fashion
- Architecture
- Religion
- Festival
- Celebration
- History
- Language
- Cultural exchange
- Folklore
- Ancestry
- Rituals
- Identity
- Society
- Cultural assimilation
- Modernization
- Folk music
- Folk art
- Sculpture
- Painting
- Performing arts
- Street art
- Cinema
- Dance
- Theater
- Foodways
- Gastronomy
- Culinary art
- Dishes
- Ingredients
- Spices
- Beverages
- Festivities
- Carnivals
- Parades
- Pageantry
- Sports
- Games
- Pastimes

Culture

Culture Speaking Prompts:

- What are some cultural traditions in your country?
- How do cultural differences affect communication?
- How does culture influence fashion trends?
- What are some common foods in your culture?
- What are some customs associated with weddings in your culture?
- How does religion influence culture?
- What are some challenges people face when adapting to a new culture?
- How does art reflect culture?
- What are some popular music genres in your culture?
- How does your culture celebrate holidays?
- How do cultural values differ between countries?
- How does globalization affect cultural diversity?
- What are some cultural stereotypes and how do they impact people?
- How does language shape culture?
- What are some important historical events that have influenced your culture?

Culture

Culture Speaking Prompts:

- How do cultural differences affect business practices?
- How do cultural attitudes toward family and community vary around the world?
- How does immigration impact culture?
- How does social media influence culture?
- How can we appreciate and learn from different cultures?

Culture

Useful Phrases:

- I'm really interested in learning about your culture. Can you tell me more about it?
- What are some customs and traditions that are important in your culture?
- How do people in your culture typically celebrate important events like weddings or birthdays?
- I'm curious about the food in your culture. Can you recommend any dishes for me to try?
- What are some typical clothing styles in your culture?
- What are some popular festivals or holidays in your culture?
- Can you explain the significance of the traditional art and music in your culture?
- How do people in your culture typically greet each other?
- What are some common gestures or body language in your culture?
- Can you share a story or legend that is important in your culture?
- How does the education system differ in your culture compared to others?

Culture

Useful Phrases:

- What are some common career paths in your culture?
- What are some important values in your culture?
- How has your culture changed over time?
- How does religion play a role in your culture?
- What is the role of family in your culture?
- What are some common superstitions in your culture?
- Can you share some slang or informal language used in your culture?
- How do people in your culture typically show respect to elders or authority figures?
- How does your culture view time and punctuality?

Culture

Writing Prompts:

- Describe a cultural event or festival that you have attended. What did you see, hear, and taste? How did you feel about the experience?
- Write about a traditional dish from your culture. What ingredients are used, and how is it prepared? What does the dish symbolize or represent in your culture?
- Share a story from your family or community that reflects a cultural value or belief. How has this story impacted your life or influenced your worldview?

Culture

Fun Culture Idioms & Phrases:

- **When in Rome, do as the Romans do** - adapt to local customs when traveling.
- **That's just the tip of the iceberg -** there's much more to explore or discover.
- **Speak of the devil** - when the person you were just talking about appears unexpectedly.
- **It's a small world after all** - when you realize how interconnected people are despite distance.
- **Actions speak louder than words** - what a person does is more important than what they say.
- **It takes two to tango** - both people in a situation are responsible for what happens.
- **Barking up the wrong tree** - pursuing the wrong idea or person.
- **All dressed up and nowhere to go** - when you're prepared but have nothing to do.
- **A picture is worth a thousand words** - an image can convey a lot of information.
- **Don't judge a book by its cover** - don't make assumptions based on appearance.

Culture

Classroom Activity:

- Activity: Cultural Guessing Game
- Objectives:
  - To help students learn and practice new vocabulary related to culture.
- Materials:
  - Index cards or pieces of paper
  - Writing materials
- Instructions:
  - In advance, prepare index cards or pieces of paper with vocabulary words related to culture. Make sure to use some of the vocabulary words provided earlier, as well as any other relevant vocabulary you want to include.
  - Divide the class into two teams.
  - Each team takes turns choosing one member to be the guesser. The guesser will sit with their back to the board or screen, where the index cards or pieces of paper with the vocabulary words are displayed.
  - The other members of the team take turns giving verbal clues to the guesser about the vocabulary word on the screen. They cannot use the word itself, any part of the word, or any translation of the word in their clues. They have one minute to give as many clues as possible.

Culture

Classroom Activity:

- Instructions (con't):
  - The guesser tries to guess the vocabulary word based on the clues given. If they guess correctly, the team earns a point. If they cannot guess, the other team gets a chance to steal the point.
  - Repeat with the other team, alternating guessers each round.
- Variations:
  - To make the game more challenging, limit the number of clues each person can give, or make the clues more difficult (e.g. only use synonyms, or use clues that are only related to one aspect of the word).
  - To make the game more collaborative, have all team members work together to give the clues, rather than taking turns.
  - To make the game more culturally specific, focus on vocabulary related to a specific culture or country (e.g. Japanese culture, Mexican culture, etc.).

Notes

Environment

Targeted Vocabulary:

- Pollution
- Emissions
- Greenhouse gases
- Carbon footprint
- Renewable energy
- Nonrenewable energy
- Fossil fuels
- Climate change
- Global warming
- Deforestation
- Endangered species
- Habitat
- Biodiversity
- Conservation
- Recycling
- Waste management
- Landfill
- Composting
- Organic
- Biodegradable
- Ecotourism
- Sustainability
- Environmentalism
- Carbon dioxide
- Ozone layer
- Acid rain
- Smog
- Natural resources
- Ecosystem
- Green technology
- Sustainability
- Ecological
- Conservationist
- Naturalist
- Renewable
- Non-toxic
- Eco-friendly
- Carbon-neutral
- Energy-efficient
- Solar power
- Wind power
- Hydroelectric power
- Geothermal energy
- Permaculture
- Soil erosion
- Wildlife habitat
- Eco-activism
- Natural fibers
- Native species
- Biodiverse

Environment

Environment Speaking Prompts:

- What are some of the biggest environmental issues facing our world today?
- How can we encourage more people to use renewable energy sources?
- What are some of the ways we can reduce our carbon footprint?
- How do you think climate change will affect our planet in the next 50 years?
- What are some of the ways we can reduce waste and increase recycling in our communities?
- How can we protect our natural resources such as forests, waterways, and oceans?
- What is your opinion on genetically modified foods and their impact on the environment?
- How can we encourage businesses to become more environmentally sustainable?
- What are some of the benefits and drawbacks of using nuclear energy as a power source?
- What are some of the ways we can reduce pollution in our cities and towns?

Environment

Environment Speaking Prompts:

- What can individuals do to help combat climate change?
- What is your opinion on the use of pesticides and their impact on the environment?
- What are some of the ways we can reduce our reliance on fossil fuels?
- How can we encourage more people to use public transportation?
- How can we ensure that our oceans are protected from pollution and overfishing?
- What are some of the ways we can reduce our water consumption?
- What is your opinion on the use of plastic bags and their impact on the environment?
- How can we encourage more people to use electric vehicles?
- What are some of the ways we can protect endangered species from extinction?
- What is your opinion on the use of wind turbines as a renewable energy source?

Environment

Useful Phrases:

- How can we reduce our carbon footprint?
- What are some environmentally-friendly habits we can adopt?
- Do you recycle? Why or why not?
- How can we conserve water in our daily lives?
- What do you think is the biggest environmental problem facing the world today?
- Have you ever participated in a beach or park cleanup? What was your experience like?
- How do you feel about using public transportation instead of driving a car?
- What are some ways we can reduce air pollution in our cities?
- Have you ever visited a national park or protected area? What did you learn?
- Do you prefer to use paper or plastic bags at the grocery store? Why?
- What do you think are the benefits of using renewable energy sources like solar and wind power?
- Have you ever volunteered for an environmental organization? What did you do?

Environment

Useful Phrases:

- How do you think climate change will affect the world in the future?
- What are some ways we can protect endangered species and their habitats?
- Have you ever planted a tree or participated in a tree-planting event? What was your experience like?
- How do you feel about genetically modified organisms (GMOs) in agriculture?
- What do you think are the advantages and disadvantages of using pesticides in farming?
- Do you try to buy products that are environmentally-friendly or sustainable? Why or why not?
- How can we reduce waste in our communities?
- Do you think that individuals or governments have a bigger role to play in protecting the environment? Why?

Environment

Writing Prompts:

- Write about a time when you felt connected to nature. What were you doing? Where were you? What did you see, hear, smell, or touch?

- Imagine you are an animal in the forest. Write a story from the animal's point of view about how humans have impacted its habitat.

- Describe a small change you can make in your daily life to be more environmentally friendly. How can this change help the planet?

Environment

Fun Environmental Idioms & Phrases:

- **To be a tree hugger** - This idiom refers to someone who is very passionate about protecting the environment and the natural world.

- **To be as busy as a bee** - This idiom refers to someone who is always working hard and constantly busy, much like a bee buzzing around gathering pollen.

- **To go green** - This idiom refers to adopting environmentally friendly practices and making efforts to reduce one's carbon footprint.

Environment

Classroom Activity:

- Activity: Eco-Inventions
- Objectives:
  - To encourage students to think creatively about the environment and come up with eco-friendly inventions.
- Instructions:
  - Start by discussing with your students the importance of protecting the environment and why it's important to come up with eco-friendly solutions.
  - Then, ask them to brainstorm some problems related to the environment (e.g. pollution, waste management, energy consumption, etc.).
  - Divide your class into groups and give each group a problem to solve.
  - Have them brainstorm ideas for an eco-friendly invention that could solve the problem they were assigned.
  - Each group should present their invention to the class and explain how it would work.
  - As a class, vote on the most creative and practical invention for each problem.
  - Finally, have your students create a drawing or model of their invention.

Environment

Classroom Activity:

This activity is not only fun and engaging, but it also promotes critical thinking, creativity, and problem-solving skills. It can also help students understand the impact of human actions on the environment and encourage them to take action to protect it.

Notes

Health

Targeted Vocabulary:

- Nutrition
- Wellness
- Hygiene
- Fitness
- Exercise
- Aerobic
- Anaerobic
- Flexibility
- Endurance
- Strength training
- Cardiovascular
- Respiratory
- Immune system
- Metabolism
- Hormones
- Digestion
- Sleep hygiene
- Stress management
- Mental health
- Substance abuse
- Healthy eating
- Well-being
- Cleanliness
- Physical condition
- Workout
- Aerobics
- Limberness
- Power
- Resistance training
- Heart health
- Breathing
- Disease resistance
- Energy conversion
- Endocrine secretions
- Metabolic processes
- Sleep habits
- Stress reduction
- Emotional wellness
- Drug addiction
- Alcoholism
- Rehabilitation
- Recovery
- Therapy
- Vaccination
- Illness
- Health care
- Symptoms
- Diagnosis
- Treatment
- Weight training

Health

Health Speaking Prompts:

- What are some ways to maintain good physical health?
- What do you do to take care of your mental health?
- What are some common health problems in your country?
- How can you prevent getting sick?
- What are some healthy eating habits?
- How can you boost your immune system?
- What are some good ways to reduce stress?
- What are some common sports injuries and how can they be prevented?
- What are some common allergies and how can they be treated?
- How can you improve your sleep?
- What are some benefits of regular exercise?
- What are some common mental health disorders and how can they be treated?
- How can you maintain good oral hygiene?
- How can you maintain good eye health?
- What are some common skin problems and how can they be treated?

Health

Health Speaking Prompts:

- What are some healthy habits to practice daily?
- What are some healthy ways to cope with illness?
- What are some important things to keep in mind when choosing a healthcare provider?
- What are some health risks associated with smoking and drinking alcohol?
- How can you maintain good overall health and well-being?

Health

Useful Phrases:

- How often do you exercise?
- What kind of exercise do you prefer?
- Do you follow a special diet?
- What do you do to stay healthy?
- Have you ever had any serious health problems?
- How often do you visit the doctor?
- Have you ever been hospitalized?
- Do you take any medication regularly?
- How do you deal with stress?
- Have you ever tried alternative medicine?
- I try to eat a balanced diet.
- I avoid eating fast food.
- I go for a walk every morning.
- I take vitamins to stay healthy.
- I try to get enough sleep every night.
- I always wear sunscreen when I go outside.
- I meditate to reduce stress.
- I don't smoke or drink alcohol.
- I am allergic to peanuts.
- I had the flu last month.

Health

Writing Prompts:

- In recent years, the use of technology in healthcare has grown rapidly. How do you think technology can improve healthcare, and what are some potential drawbacks?

- Maintaining a healthy lifestyle can be challenging, especially with a busy schedule. What are some practical tips you have for staying healthy while managing work or school responsibilities?

- Mental health is a critical aspect of overall health, yet it is often stigmatized and not given the attention it deserves. Why do you think mental health is important, and how can we raise awareness about its importance?

Health

Fun Health Idioms & Phrases:

- **An apple a day keeps the doctor away** - This means that if you eat healthy and take care of yourself, you're less likely to get sick.
- **Break a leg** - This is a phrase you say to someone before they perform or compete to wish them good luck.
- **Catch some Z's** - This means to get some sleep.
- **Fit as a fiddle** - This means to be in good physical condition.
- **Get back on your feet** - This means to recover from an illness or setback.
- **Go bananas** - This means to go crazy or act out of control.
- **In the pink** - This means to be healthy and in good condition.
- **Jump on the bandwagon** - This means to start doing something popular or trendy.
- **Kick the bucket** - This is a slang term that means to die.
- **Sick as a dog** - This means to be very sick or ill.

Health

Classroom Activity:

- Activity: Healthy Habits Charades
- Objectives:
  - To reinforce vocabulary related to healthy habits.
  - To promote discussion about healthy habits.
- Materials:
  - List of healthy habits vocabulary words (such as those provided earlier)
  - Slips of paper with different healthy habits written on them
  - Timer
  - Blank slips of paper for students to write their own healthy habit ideas
- Instructions:
  - Begin by reviewing the healthy habits vocabulary words with the class.
  - Explain that the class will be playing a game of charades to reinforce the vocabulary and promote discussion about healthy habits.
  - Divide the class into small groups and give each group a stack of slips of paper with different healthy habits written on them.
  - Set a timer for a certain amount of time (such as 1-2 minutes) for each round of charades.
  - One student from each group will take turns drawing a slip of paper and acting out the healthy habit silently while their group tries to guess what it is.

Health

Classroom Activity:

- Instructions (con't):
    - The group that correctly guesses the healthy habit within the time limit earns a point.
    - After each round, the student who acted out the healthy habit should explain why it is a healthy habit and how it can contribute to a healthy lifestyle.
    - Continue playing until all of the slips of paper have been used, or until time runs out.
    - If time allows, students can write their own healthy habit ideas on blank slips of paper and add them to the stack for future rounds.

This activity not only reinforces vocabulary related to healthy habits, but it also encourages discussion about healthy habits and allows students to share their own ideas and experiences.

Notes

Education

Targeted Vocabulary:

- Curriculum
- Syllabus
- Pedagogy
- Assessment
- Academia
- Accreditation
- Prerequisite
- Extracurricular
- Plagiarism
- Thesis
- Instruction
- Learning
- Classroom
- Teacher
- Student
- Homework
- Lecture
- Assignment
- Exam
- Degree
- Diploma
- Knowledge
- Study
- Research
- Library
- Textbook
- Notebook
- Academic
- Graduation
- Certificate
- Schooling
- Instructional
- Educational institution
- Academic program
- Classroom activities
- Learning objectives
- Academic achievement
- Intellectual development
- Pedagogical methods
- Study materials
- Intellectual capacity
- Educational development
- Academic skills
- Educational system
- Learning environment
- Educational resources
- Scholarly pursuits
- Educational training
- Intellectual pursuits
- Educational attainment

Education

Education Speaking Prompts:

- What was your favorite subject in school?
- Do you think it's important to study a second language? Why or why not?
- Have you ever taken an online course? How was your experience?
- Do you prefer to study alone or in a group? Why?
- What are some effective study habits that you use?
- What do you think is the best way to prepare for an exam?
- Do you think technology has had a positive or negative impact on education? Why?
- Have you ever had a teacher who inspired you? What did they do to inspire you?
- Do you think education should be free for everyone? Why or why not?
- What are some challenges that students face when learning a new subject?
- Do you think it's important for students to participate in extracurricular activities? Why or why not?

Education

Education Speaking Prompts:

- What are some of the benefits of studying abroad?
- Have you ever had a tutor? How was your experience?
- What do you think is the role of the teacher in the learning process?
- Do you think students should have access to electronic devices during class? Why or why not?
- What do you think are some ways to make education more engaging and enjoyable for students?
- Do you think the grading system is an accurate way to measure a student's knowledge? Why or why not?
- What are some of the differences between traditional classroom learning and online learning?
- Do you think it's important to continue learning throughout your life? Why or why not?
- What do you think is the biggest challenge facing the education system today?

Education

Useful Phrases:

- Could you explain that concept again?
- I didn't quite understand what you meant. Could you give me an example?
- What's the difference between these two terms?
- How do you pronounce this word?
- Can you give me some tips for studying for this exam?
- What are some effective study techniques?
- What resources do you recommend for learning more about this topic?
- What was the main idea of the lecture?
- Could you summarize the main points of the reading?
- What do you think about this topic?
- Do you agree or disagree with this statement?
- What are some potential benefits and drawbacks of this approach?
- How has education changed over the years?
- How important is education in your culture?
- What are some challenges students face in your country's education system?

Education

Useful Phrases:

- What are some ways technology is changing education?
- What skills do you think are most important for students to learn in school?
- What is your favorite subject? Why?
- Who is your favorite teacher? Why?
- What are your future educational goals?

Education

Writing Prompts:

- Write an essay discussing the benefits of vocational education and training, using at least five of the vocabulary words provided.
- Create a persuasive argument for why technology should play a larger role in the classroom, using at least six of the provided vocabulary words.
- Write a personal reflection on the importance of lifelong learning, using at least four of the vocabulary words provided.

Education

Fun Education Idioms & Phrases:

- **Hit the books** - to study hard, often for an exam.
- **Learn the ropes** - to learn how to do something, often a job or task.
- **Teach someone the ropes** - to show someone how to do something, often a job or task.
- **A piece of cake** - something that is easy to do or accomplish.
- **Brainstorm** - to generate ideas, often as a group.
- **A picture is worth a thousand words** - a picture can convey a lot of information or meaning.
- **Straight A's** - to receive perfect grades in all classes.
- **Burn the midnight oil** - to study or work late into the night.
- **Pass with flying colors** - to pass an exam or test with a very high score.
- **Put two and two together** - to draw an obvious conclusion from the available facts.

Education

Classroom Activity:

- Activity: Word Association
- Objectives:
  - To practice using education-related vocabulary.
  - To improve vocabulary retention.
- Materials:
  - Whiteboard or chart paper
  - Markers
- Instructions:
  - Write one education-related word on the board (e.g. "teacher").
  - Have students take turns coming up with other words that they associate with the initial word (e.g. "classroom", "chalkboard", "students", etc.).
  - Write down all the associated words on the board.
  - Repeat the process with each associated word, adding more related words to the list.
  - Once the list is long enough, have students use the words to create sentences or short paragraphs.
- Variation:
  - For an added challenge, you could have students try to use as many words from the list as possible in their sentences or paragraphs.

Education

Classroom Activity:

This activity can be adapted for different levels of proficiency by adjusting the complexity of the initial words and encouraging students to use more advanced vocabulary in their sentences or paragraphs.

Notes

Jobs and Careers

Targeted Vocabulary:

- Occupation
- Employment
- Job
- Career
- Profession
- Salary
- Wage
- Benefits
- Promotion
- Retirement
- Resume
- Cover letter
- Interview
- Employer
- Employee
- Colleague
- Workload
- Work experience
- Qualifications
- Skills
- Training
- Internship
- Networking
- Freelance
- Contract
- Part-time
- Full-time
- Job market
- Workplace
- Job security
- Position
- Title
- Company
- Industry
- Duties
- Responsibilities
- Performance
- Evaluation
- Performance review
- Growth
- Advancement
- Work environment
- Boss
- Teamwork
- Deadline
- Productivity
- Project
- Goal
- Achievement
- Work-life balance

Jobs and Careers

Jobs and Careers Speaking Prompts:

- What kind of jobs are common in your country?
- What kind of job would you like to have in the future?
- What qualifications and experience do you need to work in your chosen career?
- How important is it to choose a career you enjoy?
- What do you think are the most important qualities for success in a job?
- Have you ever worked in a job you didn't like? What was it and why didn't you like it?
- How do you feel about working in a team?
- What kind of jobs do you think will be in demand in the future?
- What do you think are the benefits and drawbacks of self-employment?
- How important is work-life balance to you?
- Have you ever had a job interview? What was it like?
- What do you think are the most important skills for a job interview?
- How do you prepare for a job interview?

Jobs and Careers

Jobs and Careers Speaking Prompts:

- What kind of questions do you think employers might ask during a job interview?
- How do you negotiate a salary for a job?
- Have you ever had a part-time job while studying? What was it like?
- How do you balance work and study?
- What kind of challenges do you think people face when they change careers?
- How can you develop your skills and experience in your current job?
- What advice would you give to someone who is looking for their first job?

Jobs and Careers

Useful Phrases:

- What kind of questions do you think employers might ask during a job interview?
- How do you negotiate a salary for a job?
- Have you ever had a part-time job while studying? What was it like?
- How do you balance work and study?
- What kind of work are you interested in?
- Do you have any work experience?
- What are your strengths and weaknesses?
- What are your long-term career goals?
- How did you find out about this job?
- Can you tell me about your previous work experience?
- What skills do you bring to the job?
- What are your salary expectations?
- Have you ever had a difficult experience at work? How did you handle it?
- Can you tell me about a project you worked on that you're particularly proud of?
- What motivates you to do your best work?

Jobs and Careers

Useful Phrases:

- What do you think sets you apart from other candidates?
- How do you handle stress and pressure at work?
- What do you know about the company and the industry it's in?
- What are some skills you want to develop in your future career?
- Can you tell me about a time when you had to solve a problem at work?
- What are some of your hobbies and interests outside of work?
- What are some of the challenges you've faced in your career so far?
- How do you stay organized and manage your time at work?
- What are some of the biggest changes you've seen in the job market over the past few years?
- How can you develop your skills and experience in your current job?
- What advice would you give to someone who is looking for their first job?

Jobs and Careers

Writing Prompts:

- Write about the pros and cons of freelancing as a career path.
- Describe a job interview you have had in the past, including the questions you were asked and how you answered them.
- Write about a time when you had to learn new skills for a job, how you went about learning them, and how you felt about the experience.

Jobs and Careers

Fun Jobs and Careers Idioms & Phrases:

- **To be a big cheese** - to be an important person in a company or organization.
- **To be a jack of all trades, master of none -** to have a wide range of skills, but not be an expert in any of them.
- **To hit the ground running** - to start a new job or project with a lot of energy and enthusiasm.
- **To climb the ladde**r - to work hard and progress through the ranks of a company or organization.
- **To be a square peg in a round hole** - to be in a job or situation that doesn't suit you.
- **To keep your nose to the grindstone** - to work hard and focus on your job or task.
- **To be a nine-to-fiver** - to have a regular job with set working hours.
- **To pass the buck** - to avoid taking responsibility for a problem or issue and pass it on to someone else.
- **To be on the same page** - to have the same understanding or agreement about something.
- **To be a workhorse** - to be a hard worker who can handle a lot of tasks and responsibilities.

Jobs and Careers

Classroom Activity:

- Activity: Guess the Job
- Objectives:
  - To practice job-related vocabulary
  - To develop critical thinking skills.
- Materials:
  - Pictures or flashcards of different professions
  - Slips of paper with the names of the professions
  - A hat or bowl to hold the slips of paper
- Instructions:
  - Show the pictures or flashcards of different professions to the students and ask them to name the profession.
  - Once the students are familiar with the different professions, write the names of the professions on slips of paper and put them in a hat or bowl.
  - Divide the class into teams and have them take turns choosing a slip of paper from the hat/bowl.
  - The team that selects a profession will then have to describe the job to the other team without saying the name of the profession. They can use any related vocabulary words to describe the job, but they cannot say the actual job name.
  - The other team must guess the profession based on the description given by the first team.
  - If the second team correctly guesses the profession, they receive a point. If they do not guess correctly, the other team receives a point.

Jobs and Careers

Classroom Activity:

- Instructions (con't):
    - Play continues with the teams taking turns choosing a slip of paper and describing the profession until all the slips have been used.
    - The team with the most points at the end of the game wins.
- Variations:
    - To make the game more challenging, you can ask the teams to describe the profession using only five or ten words.
    - For a more advanced class, you can ask the teams to give a short presentation about the profession they chose, including the job description, required skills, and education/training needed to work in that field.

Notes

Social Issues

Targeted Vocabulary:

- Diversity
- Equality
- Discrimination
- Stereotype
- Prejudice
- Racism
- Sexism
- Homophobia
- Transphobia
- Xenophobia
- Inclusion
- Exclusion
- Marginalization
- Privilege
- Oppression
- Empathy
- Compassion
- Tolerance
- Acceptance
- Social justice
- Human rights
- Advocacy
- Activism
- Protest
- Civil rights
- Injustice
- Police brutality
- Hate crime
- Bullying
- Cyberbullying
- Segregation
- Marginality
- Preconception
- Stereotyping
- Marginalization
- Intolerance
- Stigmatization
- Disenfranchisement
- Intimidation
- Alienation
- Marginalization
- Dehumanization
- Social exclusion
- Prejudgement
- Social inequality
- Economic inequality
- Poverty
- Social mobility
- Social cohesion
- Classism

Social Issues

Social Issues Speaking Prompts:

- What social issues are affecting your community?
- What do you think is the most pressing social issue in the world right now?
- What is the impact of social media on society?
- How can society tackle the problem of income inequality?
- Should the government have a role in addressing social issues, and if so, what should that role be?
- How can we raise awareness about social issues in our local community?
- What is the relationship between social issues and mental health?
- How can we reduce social isolation among elderly people in our community?
- What is the impact of poverty on society, and what can be done to address it?
- How can we promote greater diversity and inclusion in society?
- What is the impact of bullying on individuals and society?

Social Issues

Social Issues Speaking Prompts:

- Should everyone have equal access to healthcare, regardless of their socioeconomic status?
- How can society better support individuals with disabilities?
- What is the impact of climate change on society, and what can be done to address it?
- How can we promote greater gender equality in society?
- What is the relationship between social issues and crime?
- How can we promote greater understanding and tolerance between different cultures and religions?
- What is the impact of immigration on society?
- How can we reduce the stigma surrounding mental health issues?
- Should individuals be held responsible for addressing social issues, or is it primarily the responsibility of governments and institutions?

Social Issues

Useful Phrases:

- What are some current social issues that affect people in our community?
- Do you think social media has had a positive or negative impact on society?
- How can we address the issue of homelessness in our city?
- What can individuals do to promote equality and combat discrimination?
- What are some challenges faced by immigrants in our community?
- How can we encourage more people to get involved in volunteer work?
- What role can education play in addressing social issues?
- How can we ensure that everyone has access to affordable healthcare?
- What are some environmental issues that are affecting our planet?
- What can we do to reduce our carbon footprint and protect the environment?

Social Issues

Useful Phrases:

- What are some of the root causes of poverty and inequality?
- How can we create more job opportunities for people in our community?
- What is the impact of drug abuse on society?
- How can we reduce crime rates in our community?
- What can be done to address the issue of bullying in schools?
- How can we ensure that everyone has access to quality education?
- How can we promote tolerance and understanding among people of different backgrounds?
- What can be done to address the issue of domestic violence?
- How can we support mental health and well-being in our community?
- What can individuals and governments do to address the issue of income inequality?

Social Issues

Writing Prompts:

- Think about a social issue that you are passionate about, such as climate change, poverty, or education inequality. Write a persuasive essay arguing for why this issue is important and what steps should be taken to address it.

- Choose a current event related to a social issue, such as a protest or an incident of police brutality. Write a news article reporting on the event and discussing the social issue at the heart of it.

- Write a short story in which a character faces a social issue, such as discrimination or marginalization, and learns how to overcome it through empathy, compassion, or advocacy.

Social Issues

Fun Social Issues Idioms & Phrases:

- **Break the ice** - to initiate a conversation or to start a social interaction.

- **In the same boat** - to be in a similar situation or facing a similar challenge.

- **To give someone the benefit of the doubt** - to choose to believe someone's good intentions or to give them the benefit of any doubts or uncertainties.

- **To turn a blind eye** - to ignore or overlook something, usually something that is not legal or ethical.

- **To be on the same wavelength** - to understand someone else's thoughts or ideas, to be in agreement or to share a similar perspective.

- **To be in hot water** - to be in trouble or facing consequences for something.

- **To bury one's head in the sand** - to ignore or avoid a problem or difficult situation.

- **To get on someone's nerves** - to irritate or annoy someone.

Social Issues

Fun Social Issues Idioms & Phrases:

- **To have a chip on one's shoulder** - to be overly defensive or sensitive about a perceived slight or injustice.
- **To be up in arms** - to be very angry or outraged about something.

Social Issues

Classroom Activity:

- Activity: Role Play: Responding to Discrimination
- Objectives:
  - To practice responding to discriminatory situations using appropriate vocabulary and phrases.
- Materials:
  - Printed role play scenarios
  - Paper
  - Pens
- Instructions:
  - Divide the class into pairs or small groups.
  - Provide each group with a printed role play scenario that includes a discriminatory situation.
    - Example Scenario:
      - A customer at a store makes a racist comment to a sales clerk
  - Give the groups a few minutes to read and discuss the scenario.
  - Instruct each group to write a script that includes appropriate responses to the discriminatory situation.
  - After the groups have completed their scripts, have them perform their role plays in front of the class.
  - After each role play, ask the class to discuss the responses and suggest alternative ways to handle the situation.

Social Issues

Classroom Activity:

- Instruction (con't):
  - Finally, have each student write a reflection on what they learned during the activity and how they can apply it to their daily lives.

This activity helps students practice responding to discriminatory situations and reinforces their knowledge of appropriate vocabulary and phrases. It also encourages discussion and reflection on social issues, promoting empathy, tolerance, and social justice.

Notes

Entertainment

Targeted Vocabulary:

- Performer
- Audience
- Applause
- Stage
- Costume
- Script
- Props
- Rehearsal
- Scene
- Plot
- Genre
- Box office
- Screenplay
- Cast
- Crew
- Director
- Producer
- Plot twist
- Soundtrack
- Special effects
- Sequel
- Premiere
- Box office hit
- Box office flop
- Blockbuster
- Entertainer
- Performance
- Spectator
- Ratings
- Scriptwriter
- Acting
- Critic
- Dialogue
- Camera angles
- Sound design
- Film festival
- Independent film
- Documentary
- Animation
- Voice-over
- Dubbing
- Subtitles
- Score
- Improvisation
- Stand-up comedy
- Sketch comedy
- Satire
- Parody
- Musical
- Art house

Entertainment

Entertainment Speaking Prompts:

- What type of music do you enjoy listening to the most?
- What's your favorite movie genre?
- What's your favorite TV show of all time?
- Do you prefer watching movies at home or at the cinema?
- Have you ever been to a concert or music festival?
- Do you play any musical instruments?
- What's your favorite video game and why?
- What's your favorite board game or card game?
- Do you enjoy going to the theater to watch plays or musicals?
- What's the last book you read or are currently reading?
- Have you ever attended a live sports event?
- Do you prefer watching sports on TV or in person?
- What's your favorite sport to play or watch?
- Do you enjoy going to art galleries or museums?
- Who is your favorite celebrity and why?

Entertainment

Entertainment Speaking Prompts:

- What's the last movie or TV show you watched and what did you think of it?
- Have you ever watched a foreign movie or TV show with subtitles?
- Do you have a favorite comedian or stand-up comic?
- What's the last video game you played and how was your experience?
- Do you think entertainment has a positive or negative impact on society? Why or why not?

Entertainment

Useful Phrases:

- Have you seen any good movies/shows lately?
- What type of music do you enjoy listening to?
- Have you ever been to a concert?
- What's your favorite book?
- What's your favorite type of video game?
- Do you prefer watching movies at home or in a theater?
- What's your favorite TV show?
- Do you enjoy going to museums or art galleries?
- What's your favorite type of art?
- Have you ever been to a festival?
- What's your favorite type of dance?
- Do you like playing sports or watching them on TV?
- Have you ever been to a comedy show?
- What's your favorite type of comedy?
- Do you like watching musicals or plays?
- Have you ever been to a theme park?
- What's your favorite type of ride?
- Do you like watching or participating in talent shows?
- What's your favorite type of talent show?
- Have you ever been to a magic show?

Entertainment

Writing Prompts:

- Write a movie or TV show review without using the words "performer", "audience", "costume", or "special effects". What did you think of the plot and characters? Did the soundtrack enhance the viewing experience?

- Imagine you are a book critic for a popular website or newspaper. Write a review of a novel you recently read without using the words "plot", "genre", "sequel", or "box office". What were the strengths and weaknesses of the book? Did you relate to the characters or themes?

- You are a music journalist who has just attended a concert. Write a review of the concert without using the words "stage", "applause", "soundtrack", or "blockbuster". What was your overall impression of the performance? Did the artist(s) connect with the audience? How did the venue contribute to the experience?

Entertainment

Fun Entertainment Idioms & Phrases:

- **Steal the show** - to get more attention or praise than anyone or anything else in a performance or event.
- **Break a leg** - a superstitious phrase used to wish someone good luck before a performance or event.
- **Play it by ear** - to improvise or make decisions as a situation develops.
- **Let the cat out of the bag** - to reveal a secret or surprise that was supposed to be kept hidden.
- **Hit the nail on the head** - to be exactly right about something.
- **Break the ice** - to start a conversation or activity to help people relax and feel comfortable with each other.
- **Jump on the bandwagon** - to start doing or supporting something that has recently become popular.
- **Pull someone's leg** - to play a harmless joke or prank on someone.

Entertainment

Fun Entertainment Idioms & Phrases:

- **The show must go on** - a phrase used to express the idea that despite problems or difficulties, a performance or event must continue.
- **In the limelight** - to be the center of attention.

Entertainment

Classroom Activity:

- Activity: Create a Movie Pitch
- Objectives:
    - To practice using entertainment-related vocabulary.
    - To develop public speaking skills by presenting the movie pitch to the class.
    - To encourage collaboration and teamwork.
- Instructions:
    - Divide students into small groups.
    - Explain that each group will create a movie pitch for a hypothetical film. The pitch should include the following information:
        - Title of the movie
        - Genre
        - Plot summary
        - Characters
        - Setting
        - Target audience
        - Estimated budget
        - Marketing strategy
    - Encourage students to use as much entertainment-related vocabulary as possible.
    - After each group has created their movie pitch, have them present it to the class.
    - After all groups have presented, have the class vote on which movie they would most like to see based on the pitches.

Entertainment

Classroom Activity:

- Variation:
    - To add an additional challenge, you can assign each group a specific genre (e.g. horror, romance, comedy, sci-fi) or target audience (e.g. children, teens, adults) to work with.

Notes

Travel

Targeted Vocabulary:

- Itinerary
- Tourist attraction
- Souvenir
- Adventure
- Expedition
- Destination
- Voyage
- Passport
- Visa
- Boarding pass
- Luggage
- Backpack
- Guidebook
- Landmark
- Monument
- Beach
- Camping
- Hiking
- Road trip
- Cruise
- Airfare
- Hostel
- Reservation
- Jet lag
- Local cuisine
- Traveler
- Sightseeing
- Transportation
- Accommodation
- Backpacking
- Culture shock
- Tour guide
- Attractions
- Hospitality
- Travelogue
- Staycation
- Car rental
- Trip planning
- Photography
- Map
- Roadside assistance
- Travel insurance
- Exchange rate
- Language barrier
- Airport security
- In-flight service
- Budget travel
- Vacation rental
- City break
- Public transportation

Travel

Travel Speaking Prompts:

- Have you ever traveled to another country? If so, where did you go and what did you do there?
- What is the most interesting place you have ever visited?
- Have you ever experienced culture shock when traveling? If so, how did you handle it?
- Do you prefer to travel alone or with others? Why?
- What are some essential items you bring with you when traveling?
- What do you like to do when you are on vacation?
- Do you prefer to stay in hotels or hostels when traveling? Why?
- What is your favorite mode of transportation when traveling?
- What is the most beautiful place you have ever visited?
- Have you ever had a negative experience while traveling? If so, what happened?
- Do you prefer to stay in one place or travel to many different locations when on vacation?

Travel

Travel Speaking Prompts:

- What is the longest distance you have ever traveled? How did you get there?
- What is the most interesting thing you have learned while traveling?
- What is the most unique food you have ever tried while traveling?
- Have you ever taken a guided tour while traveling? If so, how was your experience?
- What is the best souvenir you have ever purchased while traveling?
- What is your favorite destination to travel to? Why?
- What are some things you do to prepare for a trip?
- Do you prefer to travel domestically or internationally? Why?
- What is the most memorable experience you have had while traveling?

Travel

Useful Phrases:

- Can you recommend any good places to visit?
- What kind of attractions are there in [destination]?
- How long does it take to get there by [plane/train/bus/car]?
- Do I need to get a visa to travel to [destination]?
- How much does it cost to stay in a hotel/hostel in [destination]?
- What's the weather like in [destination] this time of year?
- How do I get to [attraction] from here?
- Are there any famous landmarks to see in [destination]?
- What's the best way to get around [destination]?
- What's the local currency in [destination]?
- How safe is it to travel to [destination]?
- Do you have any travel tips for [destination]?
- Are there any cultural customs or traditions I should be aware of in [destination]?
- What kind of food is popular in [destination]?

Travel

Useful Phrases:

- Are there any festivals or events happening in [destination] during my visit?
- What's the best time of year to visit [destination]?
- Can you recommend any good places to eat in [destination]?
- Is it common to bargain for prices in [destination]?
- Do you have any recommendations for day trips from [destination]?
- What kind of souvenirs can I find in [destination]?

Travel

Writing Prompts:

- Write about your dream vacation. Describe where you would go, what you would do, and what you would see. Use at least 5 of the travel-related vocabulary words provided.

- Write about a memorable travel experience you've had. Describe where you went, what you did, and how it made you feel. Use at least 5 of the travel-related vocabulary words provided.

- Write a travel guide for your city or country. Include information on must-see attractions, local cuisine, and fun activities. Use at least 10 of the travel-related vocabulary words provided.

Travel

Fun Travel Idioms & Phrases:

- **Hit the road** - to begin a journey.
- **On the same wavelength** - thinking or feeling similarly to someone else.
- **Armchair traveler** - someone who enjoys reading about or watching travel experiences but does not travel themselves.
- **See the sights** - to visit and experience the famous or notable attractions of a place.
- **Travel light** - to pack only the essential items for a trip.
- **Off the beaten track** - to go to a less popular or less well-known destination.
- **Go with the flow** - to be flexible and open to change when traveling.
- **Catch a ride** - to get a ride with someone else, usually by hitchhiking or carpooling.
- **Travel bug -** a strong desire to travel and explore new places.

Travel

Classroom Activity:

- Activity: Travel Brochure Creation
- Objectives:
  - To enhance students' research and presentation skills while creating a travel brochure for a chosen destination using appropriate vocabulary and descriptive language.
- Materials:
  - Art supplies (markers, colored pencils, paper)
  - Travel brochures
  - Vocabulary lists
  - Laptops or Computers
- Instructions:
  - Divide the class into groups of 3-4 students and assign each group a destination to create a travel brochure for.
  - Provide the groups with vocabulary lists related to travel and tourism, as well as sample travel brochures for inspiration.
  - Instruct the groups to conduct research on their assigned destination and create a travel brochure that includes information such as popular attractions, cultural events, local cuisine, and accommodation options.
  - Encourage the use of descriptive language and appropriate vocabulary to make the brochures engaging and informative.

Travel

Classroom Activity:

- Instructions (con't):
    - Have each group present their travel brochure to the class and explain their choices of information and language used.
    - Optional: Have students vote on the most creative and informative travel brochure.

This activity not only allows students to practice using travel-related vocabulary and descriptive language but also encourages research and presentation skills.

Notes

Relationships

Targeted Vocabulary:

- Affection
- Attachment
- Bond
- Compatibility
- Communication
- Commitment
- Connection
- Empathy
- Intimacy
- Love
- Marriage
- Partnership
- Romance
- Trust
- Understanding
- Chemistry
- Breakup
- Infidelity
- Jealousy
- Reconciliation
- Separation
- Support
- Loyalty
- Heartache
- Resentment
- Relationship
- Companion
- Devotion
- Union
- Fidelity
- Interdependence
- Mutual
- Fondness
- Courtship
- Attachment
- Tenderness
- Kinship
- Endearment
- Adoration
- Doting
- Amicability
- Intimate
- Harmony
- Companionship
- Cohesion
- Affiliation
- Rapport
- Consistency
- Dependence
- Rapport

Relationships

Relationships Speaking Prompts:

- How do you maintain a healthy relationship with your friends or family members?
- What are some common relationship problems that people experience, and how can they be resolved?
- What qualities do you look for in a friend or romantic partner?
- How important is honesty in a relationship?
- How do you communicate effectively with your partner or friend?
- What are some common misunderstandings that can occur in relationships, and how can they be prevented?
- How do cultural differences affect relationships?
- How do you deal with conflicts in a relationship?
- How important is trust in a relationship, and how can it be built and maintained?
- How do you handle jealousy in a relationship?
- How do you set boundaries in a relationship?
- What is your view on long-distance relationships?

Relationships

Relationships Speaking Prompts:

- How do you balance your personal life and your relationships?
- How do you maintain a relationship with someone who lives far away?
- How do you handle a relationship where one person is more committed than the other?
- What are some ways to express love and affection to your partner or friend?
- How do you cope with a breakup or the end of a friendship?
- What are some common misconceptions about relationships?
- How do you deal with pressure from friends or family members to enter into a relationship?
- How do you know when it's time to end a relationship or friendship?

Relationships

Useful Phrases:

- Can you tell me about your family?
- How do you usually celebrate birthdays or special occasions in your culture?
- What kind of relationship do you have with your best friend?
- How do you meet new people?
- What do you look for in a romantic partner?
- How do you usually resolve conflicts with friends or family members?
- Can you describe a time when you helped a friend or family member in need?
- Do you think it's important to have a lot of friends, or just a few close friends?
- What are some common dating customs or traditions in your culture?
- How do you think technology has affected our relationships with others?
- Do you think it's better to be single or in a relationship? Why?

Relationships

Useful Phrases:

- How do you maintain a long-distance relationship?
- What qualities do you think are important in a good friend?
- How do you express your feelings to others?
- What are some ways you can show appreciation to someone you care about?
- Can you describe a time when you had to apologize to someone?
- How do you deal with jealousy in a relationship?
- What are some common misconceptions about relationships?
- Can you give an example of a healthy vs. an unhealthy relationship?
- How do you know when it's time to end a relationship?

Relationships

Writing Prompts:

- Write a short story about two people who are complete opposites but end up falling in love. Include descriptions of their personalities and the challenges they face in their relationship.
- Reflect on a past relationship that didn't work out. Write about what you learned from that experience and what you would do differently in your next relationship.
- Imagine you have a friend who is going through a tough time in their relationship. Write a letter to them offering advice and support, using vocabulary related to relationships.

Relationships

Fun Relationship Idioms & Phrases:

- **Lovey-dovey** - excessively affectionate or sentimental.
- **Love is blind** - used to describe the strong affection that someone feels for someone else, even if that person is not very attractive or does not have a good character.
- **Tie the knot** - to get married.
- **Heart of gold** - a kind and generous nature.
- **Head over heels** - to be deeply in love with someone.
- **Wear one's heart on one's sleeve** - to show one's emotions openly and honestly.
- **Love triangle** - a situation in which three people are involved in a romantic relationship.
- **Shot through the heart** - to feel intense emotional pain or heartbreak.
- **Cupid's arrow** - a symbol of love or the feeling of being in love.
- **Love nest** - a place where two people live or stay together, especially when they are in love.

Relationships

Classroom Activity:

- Activity: Relationship Advice Column
- Objective:
    - To practice giving advice and using relationship-related vocabulary.
- Materials:
    - Relationship Advice Column worksheet with writing prompts
    - Paper
    - Pen/Pencil
- Instructions:
    - Divide the class into pairs or small groups.
    - Explain that the class will be creating an advice column for a magazine, and that each group will be responsible for writing and answering one question about relationships.
    - Distribute the Relationship Advice Column worksheet, which includes several prompts for questions. Alternatively, you can have students come up with their own questions.
    - Have each group choose one question to answer.
    - Give the groups 10-15 minutes to discuss and write their responses.
    - After the allotted time, have each group share their question and answer with the class.
    - Encourage the class to use the vocabulary words and phrases related to relationships that they have learned.

Relationships

Classroom Activity:

- Example Questions/Prompts:
  - My partner is always on their phone and doesn't seem to have time for me. What should I do?
  - My best friend is in a relationship with someone who I don't like. Should I tell her?
  - I've been seeing someone for a few months, but I'm not sure if they're right for me. How can I figure it out?
  - My partner and I have been arguing a lot lately. How can we improve our communication?
  - My ex and I broke up a few months ago, but I still have feelings for them. What should I do?

Note: You can adjust the level of difficulty for this activity by providing more or less guidance for the vocabulary and sentence structures used in the advice column responses.

Notes

Printed in Great Britain
by Amazon